Evolution of a Queen

Myhesha Doneve

Copyright © 2023 by Myhesha Doneve

All rights reserved.

No part of this publication may be reproduced, distributed, or transmitted in any form or by any means, including photocopying, recording, or other electronic or mechanical methods, without the prior written permission of the publisher, except as permitted by U.S. copyright law.

For permission requests, contact Sovereign Noir Publications at info@sovereignnoir.com.

Print ISBN
978-1-952987-38-0

eBook ISBN
978-1-952987-39-7

Library of Congress Control Number
9781952987380

The Queen is Here
Myras Monarch

Heavy is the crown
Bedazzled thorns must be worn
The Queen is here!
Goldilocs, loaded clips in the glock
Be moved? I shall not!
I battle each war like a matriarch
A beating won't stop my steps
Too long I've lived in regret
Battles of being a mom I fight hard to protect my young
I carry them both with each arm, while my crown is still on
It gets heavy, only God can protect me, protect a Queen
Ordering my steps any which way
The enemy tries to destroy my creation, I stay grounded
Like a tree planted by water, I am life
Walking straight with a thorn on my side, I'm built for pain
No matter how many times they hurt me over and over again
I get knocked down and stand
I glow as the sun radiates power from my melanin
The Queen is here!
With a weighted crown, I ain't going nowhere
You may stand now
As I adjust my crown, head high, no bowing down
The Queen is here!
As I walk by, the flowers bloom.
May my light shine over the room!
May each word touch you as I breathe life into you
The same life that's been given to me as I walk into my destiny
You may now crown me Queen…

Decree One

Monologue of the Plethora of Personalities

Let me introduce myself. My name is Myhesha Doneve. I'm an introvert and low key shy until I get to know you. There are many layers of my being. In fact I have a few monikers. You see there's the Galactic Goddess. When you see her just know I'm in my Leo mode and want to sprinkle a little shine in everyone's life. Then there's Queen Thanos. You don't want to get her mad. When she been pushed to far her words will snap you out of her existence. Poof! You're gone. They also call me Ms. Melancholyy cause of my humble temperament. That's the part of me that just wants peace and love. Now I know what you're thinking, This woman must be crazy, schizophrenic with all these personalities. No I'm not, I just have a lot of roles I play so each one has a name.
Now Goldilocs with the Glock just might be my alter ego. She's that ride or die chick everyone wants on their roster. Why? Cause she goes to bat for those in her circle and she doesn't mind spinning the block, glocking the Glock known as her pen to put an end to drama. She's about that life and her mouth is reckless and her hands even more vicious. Test her if you want, she'll put you to sleep. Lastly, the Dark Phoenix. She is the contortionist of words who sits and observes like the Southern Oracles.
Ready to end whoever comes like a fake Neo cause she's the One who will bring peace. All these personalities make up who I am as a person. I'm potent so choose wisely cause I'm the red and the blue pill. That whiskey on ice I'll have you asking the bartender for a refill. I can leave you thirsty or quench your thirst. Anyway nice to meet you and I'm also the antidote!

From a Pawn to a Queen

I was a pawn, positioned on the battlefield to endure the unimaginable
If it wasn't because of the color of my skin, it was the reason why I was too thin
My voice was taken so my body became a weapon
I was placed in my spot for protection
Friends and foes always blocked my way
Yet I managed not to succumb to their rapture
The only wound I sustained was my heart being fractured
I wasn't built to quit, God tough not this fake stuff, plastic
I always find a way to build momentum, it's my tactic
Moving diagonally overpowering the weapons formed against me left and right
They think my ending is in sight
I'm unstoppable
I did everything they said I couldn't
I became the new nightmare on elm street
I made sure to show them that the original could never be obsolete
And when they looked up, I made it to the other side
Eyes big, mouths dropped, the look of shock
I replied, "Queen me!"

Virtuous Woman

I'm a positive influence
My sons and daughters look up to me
So I lead by example, cause I am the blueprint
I've walked through hell and tiptoed through purgatory so they don't have to
I'm the first one up, the last one to go bed
The woman in me prays diligently without ceasing
I'm full of faith
I serve God with everything in me
I seek HIS will and follow his ways
I thank Him for all the good and bad days
All my virtues are to make my family's life better
I speak words of wisdom, I encourage them, I love them
I'm hardworking, nurturing, and I fear God
So I know my soul is beautiful
A woman after God's own heart, is me
And to my future husband,
I want to help you obey God
Allow me to fan the flame of your confidence and speak loving words of encouragement to you
Cause I see God in you
Let us be like Ecclesiastes 4:9
Two are better than one because they have a good reward for their labor
And I trust you so I'm willing to surrender my heart to you and have faith in your actions
I love you unconditionally
Our house will be blessed cause we are one unit under God
The true example of the umbrella effect in marriage
God first, you second, followed by me and then the kids
So while you lead, provide and protect
I will always ensure that I nurture, teach and comfort
My love is everlasting and I'm devoted never folding
This new love God is loading in me is something I've never felt or seen

Yet, I believe God will rain down blessings
And place me with someone equally yoked
We both will be whole, then my love story with my Boaz will unfold...

Protect the King

He is dripping in melanin with honey coated chocolate lips
He deserves to be loved
I will assist him in shining his light
Cause he's been oppressed, abused due to his history
They try to keep his past a mystery
But I am here to break that curse
I will protect my king like a Dahomey Amazon warrior
I will protect my king and help him remember who he is
He is one of a kind
His words speak volumes, people are empowered
He carries the strength of a legion on men
His presence is magnetic
He is what a King is supposed to be
So I will protect him
I will stand by him, he is never alone
He will always be supported by me
Appreciated, loved, and an important part of my life
I will forever protect you and your legacy!
Cause you are a cosmic being
My beautiful mahogany King, you always treat me like a Queen
I will forever be by your side
Standing to show the world that love is always greater than hate

Strum Me

Brush your fingers softly down my spine
Allow your caress to send melodic shivers through me
With your kiss you open my gates of love
And like a guitar you strum me into a web of songs
Your touch causes me to hum notes in keys only angels should sing
With every strum I vibrate at a higher frequency
Whether high or low you know how to play me
With your heart as the percussionist
Every beat keeps me focused on you and in rhythm
Your musical composition determines my flow
Our bodies are in harmonic unison
We create a tune that rises to a crescendo
Embracing, you strum me for one last note
We exhale and our bodies go into full decrescendo

Fill Me Up God

I want more of God and less of me cause my desires could lead me on a never ending unhappy cycle
Yet, the desires of God will give me everything I want and need
So I desire God cause he fills my cup
Blessings overflowing,
Look at me I'm glowing
Independent and refusing to dim my light
I'm a vessel
Created to give life and help life prosper so I will always take a chance with God,
He's number one on my roster
His rod and his staff they comfort me
And I'm not the woman I used to be
I'm evolving
I've unlearned and learned some things
New perspective, clearer vision
I fell in love with God and realized HIS love was all I ever needed
I'm finally succeeding, no more cycles to be repeated
Generational curses are what I am breaking
A new life for me is what God is creating
And it's going to be BIG!

Heart

My heart used to bleed just for the reason to be seen
To experience love in its true form
My life has always had storms
I tried to fill it but it keeps going into cardiac arrest
I was putting the wrong puzzle pieces in my chest
Trying to fill a void but I was still left empty
So one day I fell to my knees and surrendered to God
He told me that His yoke is easy and His burden is light
God was the answer
I was gracefully broken
Words of how I feel were no longer unspoken
Given the ability to speak words of wisdom
Truth be told the answer was always inside of me
I was fearfully and wonderfully made
A poetic testimony
All because I allowed myself to be broken
I found that the greatest display of love is sacrifice
God filled that void
No longer empty I found me
My walk and talk is different
When you see me you see my light and I won't dim it for anyone
The spirit of fear has been replaced with confidence
I'm cocky with it
Protecting my peace at all costs
Call me stuck up, mean, bougie, I am
Especially when it comes to me
I bet you couldn't walk a day in my shoes
You wouldn't be able to fathom all that I had to lose
Yet God replaced what I lost ten fold
And it wasn't my soul that was sold
No clout chasing, brown nosing, or ass kissing
See this is what happens when you let go and let God
Blessings overflowing, I'm glowing and pregnant with a purpose
No reason for my heart no longer to bleed
It was all God, El Roi, cause he sees, me

Decree Two

New Number, Who Dat?

He loved me in his love language and when my heart broke, there was no compensation for the damage
In his mind he took the time to show me how much he cared
But you can't buy love and that's what he thought
I tried to effectively communicate my side but he accused me of being blind
Told me I had the audacity and that I should be grateful
All the while I just wanted him to see me, compliment me, touch me, and love me
I guess that was too much to ask
I walked away for good, I never looked back
Know your worth and create healthy boundaries I said to myself
Teach them how to treat you
Looked in the mirror, forgave myself
I love me and I come with non-negotiables
I rely on God and my faith is strong
So come at me correctly or keep it moving respectfully
This new version of me has a new mindset, better perspective
I learn then live,
Taught under false pretenses, I had to be reprogrammed
New software update cause the old me was obsolete
The new way I chose with God, I am now complete

Goldilocs

I'm Goldilocs with the glock
Glock being my pen
Ready to wear black to write your eulogy
Prepared to get with God to spin the block
To stop anyone who comes with drama
I'm the problem solver
Just know I am funeral ready
I'll read you your rights, put you to bed good night
I'll be your HUCKLEBERRY
Just start saying your Hail Marys
Cause I'm Goldilocs with the glock
Who spins the block
Here to stop, cock, lock and drop my pen to put you to an end…
The end!

Should've Been

I should've been loved
Should've been comforted and protected
Prayed for and prayed with
Instead I was used, abused and manipulated
No contraceptives given to protect me
I gave birth to a love that was still born
I still mourn
I'm full of love yet I fail to rain it out
I get depressed, feelings I'm forced to suppress
It's like a weight on my chest
Wish the cloudy days would disappear but that would mean I'd have to rain it out
And I can't stand that rain cause I'd be releasing my pain just to bottle it all back up
So I thunder and I lightning until Zeus finds me to control my weather

No Refunds

I'm the most sought after book in the library
Yet my check out card has been filled out for the last time
There won't be no refunds or returns because you took my kindness for weakness
I'm not taking back what I said in response to your blatant disrespect
You've damaged my property so fees will be assessed
Your library card has been revoked
No more trying to access my energy cause you took advantage of the good in me

No Exchanges

I was blinded by his charismatic ways until I realized that he too had his own flaws in different colors and shades
For that reason there won't be no exchanges of energy because he can't give me what I need
He's too busy trying to figure out his own speed in this world we breathe in
Yet that still doesn't negate the fact that he lacks what I need to keep me in tact
Love, affection attention and peace of mind
So I have to let him go in order to grow
Not all things are meant for forever, just seasons
Right now it's my season to grab the reins to do me and be completely free

You've Been Warned

You've been warned once
Just know the next shot will land where it is supposed to be!
You crossed the line
Took advantage of my mind so now I'm reclaiming my time
You're childish, immature and lack the brain cells to understand when to stop
Now I have to stop, cock and lock my pen to write your eulogy and put you to an end
I'm done being nice
I'm done taking the high road
You wanted me to act out of character, so I'll be your huckleberry!
Once you cross me it's alt, control, delete cause the chances of ever having me cross paths with you again is in Neveruary

Growth Of A Queen

I am always "a friend" or third wheel
Never the girlfriend or the one they want to be with
So I removed myself from the equation
Positioned myself in a situation of being single and celibate, that's my destination
Avoiding heartbreaks but I have an icebox where my heart used to be
My body is no longer a land of liberty
Cause it wasn't about being with me
They just wanted to dive in my ocean and not enjoy the beach
So like a volcano I erupted
I'm done with being disgusted
I deserve more than what I accepted
My worth just went up, I betted
To the universe, I'm forever indebted
Chakras aligned, third eye focused
The love I have for myself is potent
Me, myself and I are thick as thieves
I'm bound to succeed
I don't follow, I lead
I don't chase, I attract
If it's not adding up, I'll subtract
The old me is gone
The new me has risen from the ashes
No longer in pieces cause I found the glue
And even though some of my edges are rough and chipped I'm ok
I know that when the time is right the universe will allow for someone to love me right
All my pieces will melt correctly in place and I will finally be whole

What If

What if I could do it all over again
Go back to the time when I thought I knew what love was
Twice I said I do but almost succumbed to abuse
What if I could be a mother all over again
Take back all the milestones I missed
What if I never walked away to restart my life
I'd probably be dead, in jail or a psych ward
What if I decided to change everything to reverse the curse I thought was upon me
What if I decided not to change my past to reflect a better future
The truth is there is not a "what if" for me cause if i decided to change anything there wouldn't be Ms.Melancholyy

Fed Up : (Her side)

You fucked me like I was your woman
But the reality is, I'm not
We were just friends with benefits
And when I mentioned a relationship
You showed signs of not wanting a commitment
Yet you want me to scream your name whenever we're intimate
Nah, nigga you got me 100 ways fucked up
You see this pussy in mine
And you must be blind if you think I'm going to let you back in between my thighs
When I can see the lies in your eyes
The situation between us was stuck on repeat
I think I need a doctor to check my heartbeat
Cause when my heart skips a beat that's my receipt for all the times you hurt me
So cold I grew
I canceled my subscription from you
Your channels aren't even worth paying to see you point of view
I'm just over you...

Fed Up: (His Side)
John James the Poet

You knew I didn't want a commitment when I first made your back bend
Now you trying to do back flips, talking about relationships
I don't like boats, kayaks, and I'm too broke for a yacht
So what you not going to do is tie me on your ship when I only signed up for relations
Now you here go faking
Like if I just slide the tip in, you won't scream my name
Like the only nigga you count on for emergencies
If I kiss the nape of your neck, give your coochie a peck
Then you right back on this dick with urgency
Talking about how cold you grew when I'm the nigga that you wanted to keep you warm at night
Well this is where all that shit stops now
The only thing cold is the shoulder I'm about to give you

Patience

Slow deep breaths, meditation, mini prayers to God
I'm trying to keep my cool but my patience is wearing thin
You don't respect boundaries and act like you can't comprehend
So, off with your head!
Spinning the block, clocked my glock, you must want your clock to stop
I tried to be nice even cordial but you, you like pushing people to their limits
You know getting them out their character
So here we go...
You mad cause I cut you off
That I chose me and changed my path
Leveled up and became my own boss!
You were warned from the start
Cross me and you're dead to me
Black dress, slow singing and flower bringing
No eulogy, you just don't exist to me
I will protect my peace at all cost
You were in the presence of a Goddess
But you like to be around simple bitches and that ain't me
Forget a tax write off, you're a life write off!
You can't sing, hum, or mf skip to get my attention
May you rest in shit with the chaos that you created
I could never be jaded, your loss and I ain't sorry for your loss
I hope I live rent free in your head
And the words I've said play on repeat like a New Orleans bounce track
Guess it's time you see a chiropractor, cause I no longer have your back
Like R.Kelly said, when a woman's fed up
You no longer get the best of me
I've blocked you on everything
You're officially my past
And like a character in a movie... I got a new man, and you've been recast!

Rising Queen

It's just me, myself and I
Riding solo 'til I die
I tried, I did try, I've done enough for the ungrateful
I turned to healing instead
I'm only concerned with my own well being
I realized I have to be my own hero
No fans, no supporters
Just a lonely daughter, she be me
I turned into a lioness to protect, provide, and profess love to myself
This world offered no help and the men were no better
All they wanted was sex, no pedestal,
I was always shelved and never a priority
Played like a toy until I cut the strings and took the batteries out my back
I went from a pawn to a Queen
I'm the creator of the story
I am the theme!
Battle ready with my sword and shield
Until my fate is revealed, here I stand
Cause while they wait for my downfall
I'll never let my crown fall
Cause I'm a Queen

Decree Three

Trigger Warning

Flashing lights and all you'll see is smoke
I shouldn't have to give a warning
Yet I've been triggered
Shaking heads, face in palms, they know I'm coming
I exhale and let the fire in me loose
My face says it all
Now why you had to go and do that, huh?
My inner villain has been awaken
Some floors and bodies about to be shaking
Cause common sense ain't common
And you're the denominator that I have to put to rest
Anybody close to me knows it's best you not test me
But some people like to play with fire so it's time to get burned
I'm the first and last
Nothing you do or say can calm me down until I finish this blast of wrath
Ain't no muzzling the words I say
Usually I don't like to respond but I got time today
My attitude on Samuel Jackson and I am for real
I really meant to make your kids cry
And I damn sure not gone apologize
I need you to realize not to take my kindness for weakness, my craft as a hobby
I'm more than prepared to clock my pen
Write words in red, casting you out my life
Expeditiously, no strife
So fuck your feelings and a trigger warning
Don't play with me, play with ya maw!

My Heirs

9 to 5 to stay alive,
9 to 5 to stay alive,
Working a 9 to 5 to stay alive
You didn't ask to be here yet God saw me fit to have this title
Things haven't been easy for us but right hand on my bible,
I will always make sure you are good, it's part of my survival
These past 21 years I've learned what it means to rob Peter to pay Paul
I'll spend it all so you four don't have to fall
I rather it be me that falls to my knees praying to God to protect us please
Late nights, early mornings, doctor visits, working and playing both the parents roles
For you I'd never fold
I learned how to truly love when you all came into my life
It's like God cracked open my heart and let love pour out
I never knew I was capable to carry such a task
Yet with every smile and milestone you all have allowed me to keep on my blessed mask
Just know I will always be here for you
Holding everything together, cake batter
I'll always love you no matter what's at stake
From the depths of my soul and every ounce of breath I take

No Man, No King

How can I talk about a man being a king when all I've experienced is a man being a demon?
You see all a man ever did to me was make beg on my knees,
In my past life, I had many nights where I found myself pleading
I've been in situations that've been misleading
Cuts, bruises, my heart and body stayed bleeding
Constantly being cheated on or given a beating
Yet I'm expected to talk about a king
No, I can't do that!
Cause until I experience what a real man is, my past experiences are all I have to go on and that's a sad interpretation
Cause here I'm ruining another black man's reputation
It ain't my fault though or is it?
Cause the last time I checked I wasn't supposed to build a man, teach him how to treat a woman, teach him how to provide and protect, or help him heal
That was his parents responsibility and clearly they failed
Too busy trying to be their sons friend instead of setting the example of what it means to be a man
Just another man raised on survival and not love
Excuse me for my rant cause I just had to vent
What I endured was a case of being battered, bruised mentally, physically, emotionally, financially, and spiritually
Raising kids by myself
Robbing Peter to pay Paul got me out here wanting to be Saul
But, I digress
I just got a lot of questions that I need answered
Cause how can I talk about a king when all I've experiences are demons
In my mind I am screaming cause I know there are some real men out there
One's who really step up and out for they family
Definitely by the woman's side helping her keep her sanity
Cause honestly without a woman, there wouldn't be any humanity
Protect us women!

I mean Malcolm X said it best," The most disrespected person in America is the black woman. The most unprotected person in America is the black woman. The most neglected person in America is the Black woman."
So again I say, how can I talk about a man being king when all I've experienced are demons
I'm tired of seeing demons
So take me to God so he can introduce me to a real man

Family

Just because they're blood doesn't mean they're family
You see mine failed to provide love and protection
The miseducation of life led me down a road of hurt and strife
Past traumas caused me to use semicolons instead of periods
No I love yous, hugs or kisses
No celebrating me, invisible, milk carton missing
I decided to be distant
They've proven themselves to be my kryptonite
So out of mind and sight
Isolation became my destination
Then I had a conversation with God
I was re-educated on life,
He was waiting on me
A spiritual family is what was gifted to me
I learned that love is patient and kind
My new family welcomed me with opened arms
The abundance of love given has been mind blowing
Vulnerable I became without being ashamed
The light in me is starting to glow
My cup is overflowing with joy
My sins washed away, white as snow
I'm blooming with love and starting to show
Fears and worries are cast aside
Reborn is what I had to be
No longer alone cause I have my family standing beside me…

Love for God

I was thrown in the pit of lions, like Daniel
Realized I was the lion who had to stop lying to myself
God sent his angel to close the mouth of my fear
He showed me my true reflection
Now I'm in a new direction
From the cocoon to a butterfly
The love I have for God can never be denied
It is him that I rely, especially when I was rocking in pain
God showed up, told me I was one of his strongest soldiers
So I can stand the rain
He prepares a table before me in the presence of my enemies.
Anoints my head with oil, my cup overflows
Believe me when I say I'm ready for an OVERFLOW!
So I'm quick to listen, slow to speak and slow to become angry.
God has given me new vision, clarity, 2020
He broke me down, new foundation, new path
I'm on a new journey
I am renewed and white as snow
Through my trials and tribulations
He stood and watched over me even when I thought he was absent from me
In the end he has always covered and protected me
He was just merely waiting for me to reach my hands to thee
Now I stand here free...
So the next time someone asks why I love him
My answer will be...
Amazing grace cause he saved a wretch like me

Woman of God

She is a masterpiece of God
Steadfast and saved
This woman seeks to know God and obey him
The epitome of Proverbs 31
Her price is far above rubies
What a virtuous woman is she
She recognizes that her singleness is a gift from God and embraces it
Knowing that her body symbolizes the tree of life
She focuses on her relationship with God seeking His will and following his ways
Understanding that one day she will be discovered
This woman walks with a purpose, watches her tongue and speaks wisdom
She is a loving mother, strong, hardworking and such a positive influence
Most of all she walks in faith, not by sight and prays diligently without ever ceasing
Loving her journey, she knows she is whole
Charm is deceptive, and beauty is fleeting; but a woman who fears the Lord is to be praised
This woman of God, she is me

Man of God

It's his presence for me! This melanated man
God is first in his life and he strives to follow his will
He walks with authority
A soldier in the army of the Lord, dressed in the armor of God
doing what Ephesians 6:10-18 says
So best believe no weapon formed against him will prosper
War ready with angels on his roster
He protects and leads those he cares for
I'm intrigued and I see God's presence all over him
He's abundantly blessed, sowing and encouraging others,
I gain a better understanding, this transparency is beautiful
This man of God, I'm in awe
Watching him do the Lord's work, I see his love for the Lord
With every ounce of his being he whole-heartedly seeks God
Representing God with the help of the Holy Spirit
There's is no fear in him,
He walks by faith and never by sight
Persevering at all times so he will receive the crown of life that the Lord has promised
Man of God I see you and more importantly, God sees you too

Dear Future Husband,

Be patient with me. My past is ugly and caused me a lot of pain. I've depended on God to help me through and he showed me a new kind of love. There are days where I don't feel my best and still struggle. My anxiety, depression, and PTSD causes me to shut down at times so I am going to need for you to just encourage me.

I ask that you be my volt that holds my secrets, the arms that keep me safe and warm and a listening ear when I need to vent. Please be my best friend. I want to be completely vulnerable with you. I've been taking time to heal and break generational curses.

I asked God to order my steps, for me to be quick to listen, slow to speak and slow to become angry. I also asked him to send you to find me, your missing rib, and prepare me for you while I patiently wait.

I'm big on communication and don't like to argue. There will also be days where I need reassurance and clarity. I don't ask for much, only a little of your time and attention. More importantly, that you know God and have a relationship with him. There is so much more I want to say but I will save it for when we meet. So until then continue to let God prepare you.

Sincerely,

Your Future Wife and Queen

The Vow

In the beginning God created the heavens and the earth. On day 6 He created you from dust. Yet God knew it wouldn't be good for you to be alone. So He created me, your wife, from your rib. I am bone of your bone and flesh from your flesh. I've liked you since before we met and through God I learned to love you. I am grateful that God pushed me into orbit towards you. Cause if I had to choose someone to suffer with in life, it's you. You've loved me at my best but more importantly you loved me at my worst. Your character proved true. You've walked through hell and tiptoed through purgatory with me. You never gave up on me. Together we created our version of heaven. For that, I place this wreath upon your head. I crown you my husband, my king.

Mother's Pain

You know how hard it is for me to have to call the police on my son
I have no choice and I have to protect him from us and himself
15 with a serious mental health issue
He's losing a battle with his trauma
I swear when he looks at me, his eyes are screaming,
Mama help me!
They say it could be genetics but why do I feel like it's a curse?
My heart is hurting and the last thing I want to see is my baby in a hearse

Because of his father's father,
A history of violence followed my son like a shadow
Now he's troubled
He stays tumbling but I do my best to keep him on track
Praying yea though I walk through the valley of the shadow of death, I will fear no evil, for God is with me
Flashbacks… The day I found out I was pregnant I was quickly reminded of the kicks to my stomach from a beating his father gave me a week before.

For two months weekly doctor's visits, ultrasounds to prove his existence
God refused for him to be defeated so he stepped in and gave my son some assistance
He entered this world on an early July morning
You came here mine!
Now the hardest thing I have to do is watch him struggle
I'm struggling!
No one has the manual on being a mother
No one taught me how to do this the right way

I am doing this by myself
My heart is hurting, my mind is restless. I'm exhausted!
I suffered the same abuse but I was built not to quit
Yet he was a child not strong enough to take those hits

God gave me the strength to break us free but the damage was already done
I'm left here to pick up the pieces

PTSD gets the best of him
I swear we like Hulk and Natasha
Cause when the rage is done, it's soliloquies of apologies
And me, I am on my knees praying to God please!
He's already born with two strikes against him
At 13 he seen how mean his father could be
He said he loved and hated him in the same sentence
It hurts me that he doesn't have a positive role model
No father, no dad
This situation is a tough lesson but just know he's my blessing
I worry if I'm making the right impact in his
I do my best to show him that every man isn't bad
I fear I've failed but there's a light in him
And the confirmation is his smile
His innocence lies there

I'd go to hell and back to take away his pain
I hate that he feels that he's the blame
It's not his fault!
He was just an innocent bystander caught in the crossfire of a man who only knows survival and not love
Just know I will continue to shower you with love in ways you'd never imagine
I refuse for you to have suffer anymore damage
I'll take the pain from here.

Love, Mom

Power of a Woman

I'm tired
I'm tired of everything
From feeling rejected to unloved,
I'm there for this one and that one,
I'm helping this one and that one,
I got people depending on me
But who? Who's looking out for me?
Hell! Who can I run too?
My mother never had my back.
Even when she did, she ran and talked about me to every Tom, Dick or Jane that would listen.
Daddy was never around.
But once that liquor hit his system, he calling and crying
Better yet, he see me on the gram and wanna call and say he so proud of me, "Dis Nigga"
I've raised myself and my siblings.
I've been broken so long that what you see now is the shattered pieces that I've glued together myself.
And y'all wonder why the suicide rate is so high.
Yeah, check on your strong friends cause they don't be okay
They hurting and trying so hard not to self destruct
I walk around fake smiling
But behind closed doors I'm on my knees crying and pleading with God
I'm just trying to find me
But don't underestimate me
I'm still standing and grounded in who I am
I'm excelling instead of giving up
From being silent to inspiring, that's victory in itself
And God provided all the help
I'm a 747 to you paper airplanes
Soaring through my adversity,
I am clothed with strength and dignity,
I laugh without fear of the future
When I speak, my words are wise and I give instructions with kindness

And this little light of mine, it's the brightest
I ain't dimming it for no one
I've healed
Breaking generational curses with a purpose
Looking deeper, I found my true identity
God revealed the power within me
All because I believed in his sovereignty

Favorite Book

Allow me to read you
I want to know more than just your cover
I want to get excited to read each chapter you posses
Allow your words to flow off my lips like I'm singing the chorus to my favorite song
I wanna get lost in your illustrations
Scream at the cliff hangers at the end of your chapters
I want to know if you are fact or fiction
Whether I can understand your alternative view
I want to feel your texture as I flip through your pages
Either way I want to see if your book can stimulate my mental activity
I'm an avid reader and want nothing more than for you to enhance my vocabulary
I want to connect with the protagonist and the antagonist
Get so caught up in your story that I reach the climax with excitement
And just like a falling action, your story slows down
As I finish reading your story, I'm in awe
You are now my favorite book
So I write my review to God and pray that you are placed on his best sellers list
Thank you for being fundamental
I pray I get a chance to read you again

Lay Down

I just want to lay down
Rest my head upon your chest
Allow you to wrap me securely in your arms
Baby, you're my safe space
You calm all my anxieties and fears
You're the peace I need

You give me unconditional love
Your presence, your touch, your kiss, your smell, you...
I love the way you feed into me
Intellectually and inspirationally
Your love is intimacy

As we hold hands, interlocking your fingers with mine, we stop time
This connection between you and me, it's like we're meant to be
The way you pray for me, with me and protect me
It's love...

Guiding Light

You are the paper to my pen
With you I get to write new stories with happy endings
Whether fact or fiction
Whatever is written, is between us
You're my map and every unlocked clue leads me to your heart which is the treasure of you
You are my eyes when I can't see the best in me
My ears when I cannot hear
See you, you are the lighthouse that guides my ship home safely
Never any if's, ands, or maybes
You're my yes
Cause you've seen the worst and best parts of me
And like an anchor you stood firm and didn't let me go
Whenever I was soaked from the storms of life
Your arms kept me warm in the dead of night
You are my volt, all my secrets are safe with you
You are the glue that helped put the broken pieces of me back together
See no matter the weather you are the wind that gently touches my face
The sun light that graces my forehead with kisses
And whenever I seem to be lost your heartbeat leads me right to you
They say there's no place like home and home is where the heart is
But you, you are my home and where my heart is, there is you
Together we create a foundation that's unbreakable
No labels
We are our on genre in life
An artistic composition, we are forever written
From music notes to literature
We create masterpieces of soliloquies
Your love has me feeling free, like I'm dancing in a breeze
I close my eyes and I see you,
I feel you, hear you, I breath you
And you, you maybe the paper to my pen

But the connection between us is the ink that allows me to write about our love over and over and over again.

Decree Four

QUEEN

My light shines even below the surface
Everything the light touches is my kingdom
I'm a melanated mahogany goddess with my ancestors spirit
I break stigmas, never forgetting who I am
Mother nature, mother earth, the one true Queen
I got an army to back me, they're my ride or dies
All I want is peace
I'm a Queen of mending hearts
But If I have to come down off my throne,
I'll be the Queen of Hearts
It'll be, "Off with their heads!"
I'll just spin the block, cock the glock
Read you your rights with my pen
You'll see red, no funeral, just the end
And to those of you who want to white wash me
Please listen closely!
Wigs and makeup were created because you failed to learn the proper way to bathe
Your disease seeps from your skin
So you forced us to hide our true selves so you comfortably fit in
Yet we still shine having 40 inch hair, you love to stare
Makeup enhances our beauty
We make this shit look good!
Continue to envy us in the shadows
Call doctor Miami
Try to create yourself in our image
I would say it's a privilege but even at that you'd fail
Your revenge is to put our men in jail
Thinking women of color would fail, we rose to the top
Remember you failed to breastfeed and we raised your kids
While you used ours as bait and sold ours for a quick pay
Nah, I'm your real mother!
Try all you can to dim my light, slander my name
I'll succeed every time, you won't be able to forget my name
God proclaimed no weapon formed against me will prosper
I have all shades of melanin women on my roster

You are staring at real Queens
Bow down bitches!
Now as I ascend back to my throne just remember when you come for me you will always lose
Nothing you say or do can never silence me
I'm Queen Melancholyy who will quickly don my warrior gear
Change into Goldilocs with the glock, warrior Queen
I'll spin the block, cock and lock my pen
Eulogize, funeralize, dearly beloved we are gathered here today

Healing

No one tells you that you have to do it alone
How there's no one there to pick up and phone
Nights and days spent depending on yourself
This pain, this trauma, this healing, it's like going through withdrawals
The urge to fall back into past habits to fill the void
Nothing seems to cure the pain when your old self is being destroyed
Nightmares, seclusion to confusion everything seems to be an illusion
Having mood swings and learning new ways to do things, it's growth
Your mind, body and soul are being transformed
A new set of boundaries, morals and ideologies are conformed
You begin to see things in a new light
You've ascended mentally to a new height
Your sins have been washed away
You are pure, white as snow
The way you move forward is a different kind of flow
Those around you will see your glow
They won't be able to pinpoint the change but you will know
You will feel it when you speak, when you smile, how you talk and walk
You will even notice it in the way you dress
There will be a new confidence about you
Healing hurts but it's necessary because you're not meant to be stuck in your pain
Doing so would be inhumane
So you heal to live free and to be happy
Allowing the universe to crack open your heart, mind and soul for you to find peace
More importantly for you to find you

Love Symbols

When the universe brings us together
Be the paper, let me be the ink to your pen that seals our love with a matrimony of words
We can be run on sentences that never end
Be every adjective that leads us to the verb of love
Having no commas just a flow of music notes written for a symphony
And if I ever show you my semicolon just know it means I chose to keep flowing instead of succumbing to my fears
I took a leap of faith
Allowed the universe to seal my fate
To heaven I screamed my love for you in quotation marks with no periods
Cupid shot me in my heart then pushed me into orbit towards you
The stars and planets aligned
Our hearts intertwined into a heavenly melody
Our love played a musical for heaven and earth
A union ordained by God
We set an example of how love is greater than chaos
The universe blessed us with a shower of shooting stars as a confirmation to our fated love
And as this ink drys on this paper, we are officially one instead of two

Requited Dream

I had a thought that felt more of a dream
Of how I deserve to free myself of grief
The nightmares of hurt wishing for a knight in shining armor
Yet when it comes to love I seem to be a martyr
You see I had a dream to be the best and worst parts of me
No matter the highs or lows
I refuse to take anymore blows
I'm ready to open my heart
I'm choosing to be loved
I've decided to take a leap
Decided to speak about the things that make me weak
Even though this walk won't be brisk
Yet loving my true essence has been worth the wait
No longer being stubborn
I'm leaving everything up to fate
One day I will actually be able to say, "Save the Date!"
My optimism rising, heart palpitations remind me to ignore negative temptations
Love is the only tingling sensation I want
I just want butterflies from looking into my Boaz's eyes
I want a love that won't be denied
I've finally forgiven myself
I've died enough times and reached nirvana
I am the best and worst parts of myself
I am more than worthy of love and to be loved
My dream will transform beyond a thought
Just as I have transformed into a butterfly...

Insecurities

He had a habit of being facetious
Treating women like a thesis
But the hypothesis is, he has daddy issues
Never taught how to provide and protect
Daddy taught him how to be absent or abusive
So he grows up treating women like their useless
Not to mention being narcissistic, unaffectionate, and emotionally unavailable
And you wonder why we say niggas ain't shit
But wait,
Some of us women are no better
You see some of us have mommy issues
Yeah, I said it!
Mommy issues cause we tend to be overbearing
So we over achieve
Leading us to low self esteem and mental health issues
We end up looking for love in all the wrong places
Dressing provocative to get noticed
Body enhancements and jealousy is a hell of a drug
All for likes and smiles on mens faces
And you wonder why they call us gold diggers and hoes
At the end of the day people want to show and tell
All on social media showing their tail
Telling tall tales just to get noticed
Not realizing they need to take a look in the mirror and get focused
But who am I to judge?
I got my own demons I'm battling
I walk confident, smile on my face with my warrior gear on
Focused on healing and breaking generational curses
Cause I've done enough for the ungrateful
My focus is now on me
Pouring all that love and attention on the woman I'm becoming

Purpose In Pain

I'm in the most pain at night
When I should be winding down to sleep
My mind races like ships fleeting
The pain of life leaves my heart bleeding
Blow after blow my senses are shattered
Why won't death come to rescue me?
Especially since it won't let happiness come be with me
This vessel of mine, the light in me finds it hard to shine
Never experienced love the right way
So I keep my mind busy with distractions until it's capable of subtracting the pain permanently
I refuse to let my mind be the devil's playground
I stay knees, hands, feet and face down in prayer until I am renewed into a new woman
When I look in the mirror I'm not used to the woman I am seeing
Home doesn't feel like home, when I'm there my mind is blown from the fragments of my broken past
Therapy has me healing traumas and breaking generational curses but why did I have to be the chosen one?
My life has failed to be fun
No bed of roses, no good ship lollipop
I sit here waiting for the pain to stop
Tic tock, tic tock is what I hear from the clock
I wonder where time is going cause they say it heals all wounds
All it's done for me is allowed me to reflect so I don't repeat my past transgressions
In the end I've learned a lot of lessons
One, fear no man but God
Two, keep your life private
Three, think before you act, even consulting God before you get off track
Four, what is for you will be for you
Five, lead don't follow, and most importantly stay true to you
No one can be me
So each morning that I am allowed to see the light of day
I pray to be a better version of what I was yesterday

And even though I struggle, cry and have pain
God's not through with me yet, so I don't mind a little rain

Dream

I go to my dreams cause reality can't hurt me there
In the waking world, people are the nightmares on every street
Yet when I sleep, me and death greet, and it's not my soul it wants to reap
Instead it wants peace cause life always brings it one last breath
When I sleep I have peace
I have conversations with the Sand Man while building sandcastles creating my own land
I'm the Queen in my dream
No Alice in Wonderland or Queen of hearts
Just peace in these dreams cause the world is not what it seems
Yet while I'm awake, I pray diligently
The matrix we're in is full of sin so no one can cast the first stone
Click my heels three times, Dorothy, there's no place like home
In my bed to sleep so my mind can run free
Where I can mentally be me

His Love Language

I want to spend time with you
You know, interlock my fingers with yours
Smell you, touch you, caress your beard and kiss you
I want to kiss your neck, bite your ear and love all over you
I just want to be in your presence
Allow you to feel safe in mine
To wrap my arms around you and hug you tightly
Be that blanket that keeps you warm
Let's lay under the sheets in the dark with the candles lit
I'll rub your back and whisper sweet nothings in your ear
Let's converse about the universe, life and our future plans
Let's laugh until we cry, let's just hold hands
And as we stare into each others eyes
I will speak life into you
Remember these words: you are loved, needed, appreciated and important
Allow me to spend time with you
I just want to love you in your love language

Pen to Paper

It's something about putting pen to paper and releasing words
Letting my feelings bleed to allow people to read my emotions
Changing phases like the moon
Cause when my heart breaks, there's no compensation for the damages
The thoughts that have been keeping me bound are now dead to me
Just written soliloquies of memories
See there's something about pen and paper that allows me to be the creator
Whether fact or fictional, I create the narrative
You want to sleep? Let me write you a dream
Happily ever after? I'll write you a love story down to the your vows
A romantic? I'll poem all over you
But piss me off and I'll rain down poetry like you've never seen
I'll expose all your truths
So don't play with me or I'll turn you into a poem
That pen and paper, their both electric
Like thunder and lightning, my writing comes in all forms of weather
Shooting arrows at rain clouds to bring new growth in
My pen is to paper like mouth is to ear
And my tongue is like the pen of a skillful poet,
God wrote this
And you can write me off but all that means is your heart is off
My tongue is God's pen, He is the Alpha and the Omega... Amen

Solar Love

I don't want to hide
I want you to see my true side
The one that is rarely seen
I want to strip down in your presence
Let you see my glowing essence
Everything about you gives me solace
I'm grounded, rooted in your love
The sun set on you and I became your moon
Whenever we kiss, my body goes into a full eclipse
The frequency of your love carries me away
We connect like atoms merging
As we embrace, you swing my hips as if they bear the rings of Mama Saturn
Let's align our chakras
Allow my womb to be the portal to a new realm
You know your constellations circulate me
The planets have aligned and our love is in full bloom
When we connect it's like a spiritual transcendence
This evolution of we, births soliloquies of synchronicities
We flow freely and gravity can't hold us down
I'm never off course when I orbit with you
Stretching my vertebrae, I rotate on your axis
Shooting stars confirm that our beings were meant to be
We possess all the elements of L.O.V.E
So let me strip down in your presence
Show you my glowing essence
I want you to see my true side
I don't want to hide

Endangered Species

I am an endangered species
Look at me, I'm a black woman
Placed on a stage naked, a window display
Poked and prodded to be sold as property
I have been exploited and fetishized
It's only right I call myself an artist
And damn right!, I'm sensitive about my shit
Give me life or give me liberty
Either way each comes with a price
So I'll do my own bidding
God is always with me, I stay winning
I'm an endangered species
I carry the Eve gene and yes I am every Caucasians dream cause they want to be me
Melanated, thick hips and thighs
Booty for days and the curl of my lips
That twinkle in my eyes, the universe itself
And lets not forget my hair, it connects me to the divine
I am an endangered species
Instead of worshiping God with me you went to war on me
But like the phenomenal woman I am
I rose from my oppression
Some might say I've been resurrected
I was an endangered species
But the predator became the prey
I took my place on the throne
And now the endangered are dangerous, so…run!

Testimony

Picking up the pieces
Questions running through my mind, they're misleading
So I paused, prayed and waited
Allowing God to refocus me
With Him I have 20/20 vision
I'm on a mission, so I surrender to His will
He paid the price for it all, so I don't have a bill
He is the bread of life so I'm always spiritually fed
Looking to God for understanding,
I asked God why he gave me a big heart
Cause I love hard yet it isn't always reciprocated
He showed me I allowed myself to be easily manipulated
I broke my own heart and that hurt more than anything
Discernment, He revealed is what I needed
Develop that and I won't find myself in situations that are deceiving
Forgiving myself was another lesson
Through all the testing there was a blessing
No more searching for myself or being a puppet with strings
God showed me my true identity
Created in his likeness, I am part of his entity
All my trials and tribulations
He explained to me this was my last season of pain
So I'll continue to carry my umbrella cause I don't mind the rain
My tests became testimonies and my mess became a message
And through it remembered that he loves and he cares
So he'll never put more on me than I can bear

Roar of my Pen

The roar of my pen are words unspoken by the silent
It articulates the past and present of feelings and emotions
Giving life to experiences
Never shying away from the truth
This pens roar is on the hunt
Never violent, not like a thief in the night
My pen comes in the daylight, no flash light
When you see it, just know it's been summoned
Tasked to write a eulogies or soliloquies
It's destination is to let the ink of words flow freely
My pens roar is loud
When it speaks people stand at attention and listen
It's majestic, coming in all forms of stanzas, ballads, sonnets to haikus
When it's done inking its heart out, it lets me speak
And my roar is even louder
Sending shock waves of eargasms
My voice will have you screaming
"Rewind!" followed by claps and standing ovations
Sending spine chilling sensations
For my tongue is like the pen of a skillful poet
God bestowed it
I'm not just a writer, I'm a composer!
Paper to pen, forever a poet
Like fingers stroking a stringed instrument
Music notes turned to DNA
Poetry runs through my veins
Sometimes it's packed with rage
But just know when my pen roars
It's been let out the cage
Another prey just slayed

My Poetry

My poetry is the day I was born
My happy and sad moments
All the times I was angry
All the times I cried
My poetry is my hurt and pain
Every experience, emotion and feeling
The hugs and kisses I never received
It's the times I wasn't celebrated
Poetry is me not being told I love you
The abuse I allowed cause I didn't know any better
Its being a domestic violence survivor
All the times I was silent when I should've spoken up
Its me taking my voice back
My poetry is how I Olivia Pope'd myself
It's my therapy, PTSD, anxiety, depression and trauma
My poetry is my healing
Is all the times I fell to my knees and asked God for forgiveness
The many times I told God to lead and I'll just follow
My poetry is feeling the love of God
The feeling I felt when I understood what love was
When I forgave and loved myself
My poetry is my peace
Is the birth of my children
Poetry his watching them grow and flourish
My poetry is my granddaughters
To another generation of strong black women
It's me breaking generational curses
Is my accomplishments and overcoming adversity
My poetry is every word and sentence I write
Every poem I recite
My poetry is every time I step on stage
My poetry is me
My poetry is Myhesha Doneve

Rebirth

In 2022 I was reborn
I broke my own levees
Released the pain deep within
No longer flooded by the debris from my past
I am now exposed
Eyes wide open, I'm disclosed
My shattered pieces reflected my painful memories
Vulnerable and unguarded
I D'jango'd myself to freedom
No longer a slave at Candy Land
No more abuse from any man
God created me in His image
I am a new woman
From nothing to something
Nonexistent to blooming
New phase, full moon
I'm pregnant with a purpose
I've seen death so much that I wanted it to come rescue me
Then God showed me he had a better plan for me
Breaking generational curses and healing traumas
Blessings and confessions
Healing hurts but it's necessary
I used to be afraid of my reflection
Yet self was ashamed of me
All cause I afraid of what I'd truly be
But from a pawn to a Queen
I maneuvered my way through the scene
I'm seamless
I know God sees this, my growth
This rose that grew from the concrete
From the darkness I was created and from the darkness I bloomed
That's how I came here in early August from the womb

Return of the Locs

Allow me to reintroduce myself.
Goldilocs with the glock, that's my pen
I have a habit of writing people's eulogies, you know, the end
Took a break to recalibrate my equilibrium and align my chakras
But lately my trigger finger been itching
Slow your roll if you come around me cause I might leave you twitch"
You know reboot your system cause you came at me glitchin'
Be nice and I won't ask twice
I'll just quietly drape myself in a black
Full character, Goldilocs with the glock
Spin the block, cock my pen, in Jesus name we pray…Amen

Eulogy

Dearly beloved we are gathered here today to say my final goodbyes to my trauma
From all the words that were left unsaid to the things that made me feel dead
I'm free now so you can no longer destroy me
I came from a history of violence that tried to silence me
My trauma took my voice like Ursula did Ariel
Yet I stood up from my burial and refused to lay lifeless
I took my voice back and stood tall
And to the pain I hid in shame, you had me shackled
Yes you got the best of me for a minute
You even had me bound
But like Popeye coming to save Olive Oyl, I ate my spinach
So here I come to save my own day
I'm done crying in the car
Done being depressed, done with having scars
Ready or not, I can't hide cause my trauma finds me and takes me slowly down the path of no return
I'm left feeling stuck
It's good me vs bad me
Pick a side, pick a side
I can't decide cause both are strong
Bad memories override the good in me
Then my heart begins to sing cause I've got love all over me
I don't want to give up cause I have something inside of me that needs to be released
So I dress in black, sip my tea and do the shadow work to purge myself
I allow myself to regurgitate all that tried to kill me of my true being
Close my eyes, take a deep breath and exhale

I know this time I didn't fail
I succeeded in shedding the old me cause now I'm free
So ashes to ashes and dust to dust
The trauma of my past is dead now
The new me flourishing was a must

The Benediction

Thank you for taking the time to read my book. For momentarily peeking into the window of my life and being my audience. You are all appreciated and I pray you enjoyed this poetic journey. Remember to always be YOU! Don't let anyone dim your light or take your voice. Stay true to yourself and let God lead the way.

I also extend a very special thank you to my family. Thank you for being my audience and helping me name some of the poems. Also for always encouraging me, speaking life into me, and for pushing my pen.

www.ingramcontent.com/pod-product-compliance
Lightning Source LLC
Chambersburg PA
CBHW041326110526
44592CB00021B/2842